D0778555

COMPARING
RELIGIONS

Food and Fasting

Fasting

Deirdre Burke

Thomson Learning
New York

Comparing Religions

Birth Customs
Death Customs
Food and Fasting
Initiation Customs
Marriage Customs
Pilgrimages and Journeys

About this book

This book looks at issues concerning food and its place in the lives of believers from six major religious traditions. Food is used in many customs, including weekly services and special festivals.

Food laws spring from fundamental beliefs in many religions and **Food and Fasting** provides an introduction to these beliefs. Each chapter deals with one aspect of eating or fasting, so that readers may compare different attitudes and beliefs closely. The importance of fasting in some religions and the many symbolic uses of food are included to show the different ways in which people remember their god through eating or not eating.

First published in the
United States in 1993 by
Thomson Learning
115 Fifth Avenue
New York, NY 10003

First published in 1992 by
Wayland (Publishers) Ltd.

Cataloging-in-Publication Data applied for

ISBN: 1-56847-034-7

Printed in Italy

Contents

Introduction 4

What to eat 6

How to eat 13

Food at places of worship 16

Food and festivals 22

When not to eat 29

Glossary 30

Books to read 31

Index 32

Words that appear in **bold** in the text are explained in the glossary on page 30.

Introduction

When children are asked what they would like for lunch, their answers sometimes depend on their religious beliefs.

"Cheeseburger and chips for me, please," says Kelly, a Roman Catholic.

"I don't want a cheeseburger," answers Harpreet, a Sikh. "It is made from beef and I don't eat cows, so I'll have a vegetable samosa."

"Me next!" says Samina, a Muslim girl. "I am going to have the **halal** chicken. I don't eat pork or meat that is not halal."

"I'll have a vegetable samosa, too," says Jason, a Hindu. "I don't want the cheeseburger since the cow is a holy animal."

"I can't eat the cheeseburger either," says Daniel, a Jewish boy, "The meat is not **kosher,** and I don't eat meat and cheese together."

Do you and your friends have talks like this at your meal times? If you do, you may already know that Sikhs and Hindus do not eat beef, and that Muslims and Jews will not eat pork. Do you have dietary restrictions like these?

Have you ever thought about why you eat some foods and not others? Do

Above Children at this school are able to choose meals that are halal or **vegetarian.**

you know why some people never eat certain foods, or why special foods are eaten at important times of the year? Perhaps the most interesting question is "Why do some people go without food by fasting?"

The answers to some of these questions will become clear as we investigate religious customs about food.

What we eat

Left   Do your mealtimes look like this? Imagine what it would be like to have dinner with a family whose ideas about food are different than yours.

"Would you like something to eat?" You have probably been asked this question hundreds of times. If you are hungry you might just say "Yes please," knowing that your parents will give you good food. Some people do not eat certain foods because they are bad for their health. Throughout the world, you will also find people who eat some foods and not others because of their religion.

Food laws and beliefs

Many religions have laws that state what food people can eat and how it should be prepared. Some of these laws come from the belief that certain foods are unclean, and others stem from the belief that certain foods are holy.

Buddhists do not have specific laws concerning food, but general laws called precepts are followed. The first of these precepts is not to kill or harm any living creature. This means that it is a sin to kill animals, so many Buddhists are vegetarians. They do not eat meat.

Beliefs about food

The Hindu tradition teaches that because certain animals are holy and special they should not be killed and eaten. Jason said that he cannot eat beef because it is the meat of a cow, which is a holy animal to Hindus. In one Hindu holy book it is written, "All who eat the flesh or permit the **slaughter** of cows will rot in hell for as many years as there are hairs on the body of the cow."

Like Buddhists, Hindus also respect animals. They believe that each living

Below Buddhist monks eat only one meal a day. They eat only enough food to keep their bodies healthy, and they do not eat after midday so that they can meditate without feeling drowsy.

thing has a soul that will be reborn in another body. Hindus influenced Sikh eating habits. Sikhs do not eat beef, even though the teachings of their **gurus** do not forbid it.

Most Christian religions do not have food laws. The way Christians think of food was shaped by a special dream that St. Peter had. In this vision Peter was shown animals and told to eat. At first he hesitated because he had been brought up as a Jew and believed that some animals were unclean. He was told in the dream that it is not what you eat that makes you unclean but your own thoughts and actions.

Some religions say that certain animals are unclean and should not be eaten. This is why Muslims and Jews do not eat pork. Samina says, "You shoud not eat

Left To Muslims and Jews, the pig is an unclean animal.

Jason, a Hindu, aged seven: "We can't eat cows because they are holy—they were created at the beginning of time. Also, I like to drink milk, so I don't want to eat cows if they give me milk."

food with animal fat in it, or eat pig. We cannot even touch pigs."

Food that Muslims eat is called halal, which means food that is permitted. Food that is not permitted is called **haram.** Halal food does not have any pig products in it. This covers foods like bread, cakes, and cookies that could have animal fat in them. It is also important that animals permitted be killed and prepared in the correct way.

Some branches of the Jewish religion have complex rules about food. In one Jewish holy book, the Torah, there are laws that state which animals, fish, birds, and insects are clean. Animals are clean if they chew cud (this means they have more than one stomach for digesting plants), and have a cloven (divided) hoof. Sheep and goats are clean, while the pig, camel, and hippopotamus are unclean. Some Jews explain that the laws forbid all animals with evil instincts—animals that eat each other or have dirty habits like eating waste. The belief is that people should shun these qualities wherever they occur.

Some religions also have rules on how food should be prepared. These laws may cover how to kill the animal. Samina says, "When we kill a chicken we say a prayer to thank Allah (God) for the food, so that it will be fresh and not poisonous."

Killed in the name of God

Jews, Muslims, and Sikhs all have their own ways of killing animals. In each religion though, the animal is killed by one single cut with a knife and a special prayer is said. The Sikh prayer is "Truth is immortal," and this way of killing is known as *Jhatka*.

For Muslims halal food must be killed and prepared in the correct way. Without the right prayer, a chicken will be haram. Once an animal has been killed, all the blood must be drained from the body. Halal meat is sold at shops which display the sign "Halal."

Many Jews only eat meat that is kosher. This means that the meat is from a clean animal that was killed in the correct way and drained of blood. This method of slaughter is known as *Shehitah*.

Many people think ritual slaughter is cruel, since the animals are not stunned before they are killed. However, for those who slaughter animals like this, the prayer shows that they only kill God's creatures in the way that they believe God told them to. It shows they do not take the killing of any of God's creatures lightly.

Special preparation of food

The Hindu religion has rules saying who may prepare food for others. Some Hindus still follow rules that divide

Above In a halal butcher's stall the meat has been prepared according to Muslim rules.

Above The Hindu family in India makes sure that the ground and the banana leaves are clean before they eat.

people into **castes** and keep those of different castes from eating with each other. Hindus take great care to keep food away from dirt, and to make sure that leftover food is thrown away, to prevent the spread of germs.

Many religious people say a prayer while preparing food. Harpreet's mother says "God is one" when she is preparing food. She also covers her head before cooking or serving food. Other Sikhs may take a bath before cooking to make sure that they are clean. Traditions also say that there should be no gossip when food is prepared in the **gurdwara.**

The Jewish food laws put food that is allowed into three catagories: meat; dairy products, such as milk and butter; and parve, such as fruit and vegetables. Meat needs to be carefully prepared with salt to wash out the blood. Meat and dairy must never be cooked or eaten together. Under these rules, one cannot eat buttered potatoes with roast chicken nor have ice cream afterward. Some Jewish homes have two sinks, two counters, two stoves, and at least two sets of pots, pans, silverware, and china. This way meat and dairy foods are not prepared or served using the same wares.

Food laws have reasons

There are many reasons why these laws are important. Some religions believe that certain foods are unclean and should not be eaten. Religions that only allow the killing of animals in a certain way may be trying to make sure that believers always remember God. Those religions, like Islam and Judaism, that do not allow followers to eat blood may be trying to create a horror of bloodshed. Some religions use food laws to prevent followers from eating with people who do not belong to the same religion.

Above Sikh women cover their heads and say prayers before they prepare food in the gurdwara.

How to eat

What do you do before you eat? Have you seen other people doing something special before they eat?

Words and actions before eating

Many people wash their hands and say special words before and after eating. Almost everyone washes their hands before eating, to prevent germs from entering the body. For people who belong to a religion it may be important to also say special words before they eat a meal.

Some Jews say special **blessings** when eating particular foods—the number of blessings depends on what they are eating. Blessings are a way of saying that something is holy and belongs to God. Saying blessings is how these Jews remember God and the things that God has done for them. **Orthodox Jews** tend to follow their traditions closely. There is a long prayer for meals eaten by three or more men and a shorter one for fewer than three. Part of the shorter prayer shows how Jews are grateful to God: "Blessed are you, O Lord our God, King of the Universe, who feeds the whole world with goodness." The blessing also reminds the people

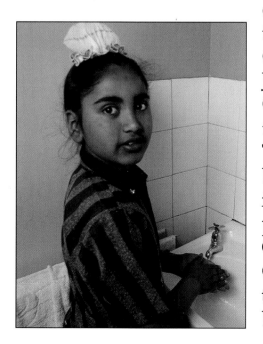

Below Harpreet, a Sikh boy, washes his hands before eating.

James, a Christian, aged nine, describes grace: "Saying grace is a good idea as it blesses the food, which means that the food has been made special by Jesus. After eating we say 'Thank you God for this wonderful food.'"

of what God has done for them in the past and how they are saying the same words their **ancestors** said in the past.

Christians often say **grace** before a meal. It is a way of thanking God for the gift of food and making eating special. This grace is more than 100 yeard old: "Bless us, O Lord, and these thy gifts, which we are about to receive of thy bounty, through Christ our Lord. Amen." These special words help Christians to remember their belief that God created them and provides them with all they need.

Hindus and Sikhs do not have to say any set prayers before meals, but many do. Some of these prayers are short, like the one Sikhs say in the gurdwara before eating. They cover their heads, as a sign of respect, then hold a **chappati** in their hands and say the prayer. For special occasions at the gurdwara a

Right This Hindu family sprinkles water around the food before eating.

Below These Indian women make sure that they only use the right hand for eating. The right hand is used only for clean activities.

longer prayer may be said: "God is the provider for everyone, there is no shortage." At home a short prayer, "God is one," may be said.

A custom that many Hindus follow at home is to sprinkle water over the food and ask God to bless it. A small amount of each food may be taken from the table and given to animals or birds.

After eating, most people want to give thanks for the food, just as you probably say a thank you when people give you things. For Muslims, Hindus, and Sikhs it is important to wash their hands after eating. This custom probably comes from using fingers, not forks, for eating.

The next time you sit down to eat a meal think about the things that some religious people do to make eating special.

Food at places of worship

Offering and sharing food

What do people eat in places of worship? Sharing food is important to people. Some religions always have food to offer in their place of worship. Others use food during or after the main service.

In Hindu temples the priest will offer the food—usually water, milk, sweets,

Below After the food has been offered during the Hindu "fire service," it will be given to worshipers along with fruit, nuts, and sweets that have been blessed.

and fruit—during the service, which may take place twice a day. The food is placed on a tray with **purified** water, **incense**, and a lamp. The food is offered to the gods and then given to the worshipers. It becomes *prasad* (holy food) when it is shared. Water and milk are placed in the worshiper's right hand with a spoon. Many Hindu temples have a special weekly service. This "fire service" is called "*Havan*," and it may be followed by a **communal** vegetarian meal.

Communal meals—eating together

The communal meal is very important in Sikhism. Food given by worshipers is cooked by volunteers in the communal

Below The *kirpan* is one of the five signs that a Sikh wears. Here it is used to stir the ingredients of the *karah parshad.*

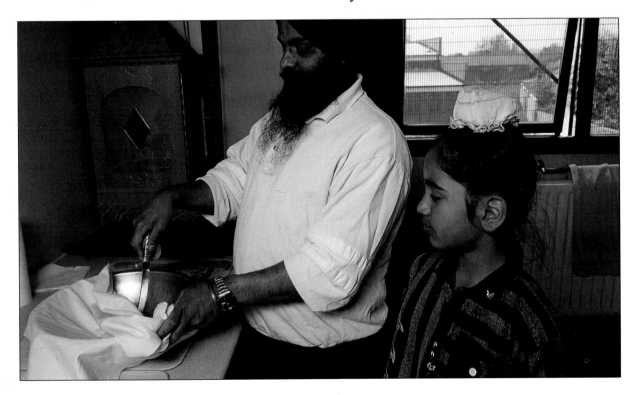

Uma, a Sikh girl, aged eight, is being served food that everyone eats together in the gurdwara:
"After the service at the gurdwara, everyone can share a meal in the kitchen, called the *guru ka langa*. It means the guru's kitchen. Lots of people help make the food, then anyone can join in when we eat it."

kitchen, called the *guru ka langa*. This means the guru's kitchen. Many Sikhs help out by preparing, cooking, and serving the food. Hymns are sung and prayers are chanted while the food is being prepared. A small portion of each food cooked is blessed by offering it to Nam (God). This food is then mixed in with the rest of the food, which blesses the whole meal.

The Sikh teacher Guru Nanak began the custom of communal eating in the gurdwara to show that everyone is equal. The food supplied shows that Nam provides for all the needs of the people, in worship and in eating food. The communal idea is also shown in the sharing of *karah parshad*, which is a mixture of flour, butter, sugar, and water. This is prepared in a ritual way. A prayer is said and a special sword called the

Right Helpers in a gurdwara hand out portions of *karah parshad* to everyone there.

kirpan is used to mix the ingredients together. This **symbolizes** the strength that the community gets from worshiping and eating together, as members of one family.

Symbolic eating

At the heart of Christian worship is the **Eucharist,** which is also called Holy Communion, the Lord's Supper, or the Mass. At this time, Christians remember the last supper that Jesus shared with his disciples (followers). At this supper Jesus broke bread and poured wine in a simple ceremony, which he told his followers to do in memory of him. Many Christians take Holy Communion as a symbol of the death and **resurrection** of Jesus, so that the gifts of the bread and the wine "may be to us his body and his blood."

Many Christians believe that the bread and wine actually change into the body and blood of Jesus. Some Catholics fast before taking communion because they do not want the holy food to come into contact with ordinary food in their stomachs.

The breaking and sharing of bread is also important in Judaism. On *Shabbat* (the weekly day of rest) the Jewish community will make *kiddush*, a ceremony in which bread and wine are blessed. The bread is usually a braided loaf called *challah*. Two loaves are used to remember the two portions of manna,

Above This Christian minister places the communion bread in worshipers' mouths. In many churches the bread is put into the hands of the worshiper.

Right A special *challah* is used at a Jewish wedding. The bread has salt sprinkled on it before it is eaten.

which was the special food that the Israelites were given when they were in the wilderness. *Kiddush*, which means making holy, takes place in homes for the three meals of *Shabbat*. In the synagogue, the congregation will make a *kiddush* together on Friday evening and Saturday morning.

Daniel, a Jew, aged ten: "Every Friday night we have the *Shabbat* meal. The grown-ups bless and drink a glass of wine. Under the cloth on this table is a special bread called *challah*. It is braided and there are two loaves that are blessed and eaten."

Food and festivals

Festivals are fun times set aside for remembering important people and events. At such special times people usually celebrate by eating special foods. Do you celebrate a festival where you eat special food? Some festivals have their own flavor, and when people think of the festival they often think of the foods that are eaten. Can you think of any foods that are eaten at festivals?

Hidden messages in food

Do you know why some people eat mince pies at Christmas, the time when Christians celebrate the birth of Jesus? When he was born, Jesus's crib was a *manager*, and hundreds of years ago mince pies were called "crib pies." They were made in the shape of a manger with a pastry baby on top.

Below Kelly, a Christian, shows her friends a crib pie—a mince pie with a pastry baby on top.

Crosses and eggs

Easter is another Christian festival that has special foods. Hot cross buns are traditionally eaten on Good Friday, the day on which Jesus died. He was killed by being nailed to a cross and left to die. The cross on the buns reminds Christians of how Jesus died. The spices in the buns remind them of the spices that were

Above The foods eaten at the Seder meal all have special meanings. They remind Jews of the Israelites' escape from slavery in Egypt.

used to prepare Jesus's body for the tomb.

Some Christians eat Easter eggs. Eggs are a symbol of new life and of the resurrection of Jesus. Christians believe that Jesus came back to life three days after he died: this is called the resurrection. They eat Easter eggs to celebrate his new life.

Remembering events through food

Jews also have special foods that are eaten only at certain festivals. At Passover a special meal called the Seder is eaten. Children ask why they only eat *matzah* (flat bread that has no yeast in it) when at other times they can eat bread with yeast. The answer to this question takes them back over three thousand years to the time of their **Exodus** from Egypt. Before their escape, the people of Israel worked as slaves in Egypt. The Seder commemorates their experiences.

Food is dipped in salt to remember the tears they cried as slaves. Bitter herbs recall the bitterness of slavery. Unleaven bread or *matzah* is eaten because the Israelites could not wait for the bread to rise when they hurried away from Egypt. Fresh greens, a symbol of spring and new life, remind people that the Jews were given the chance to start a new and free life in obedience to God's commands.

Other Jewish festivals have special foods associated with the theme of the festival. At Hanukkah, the "miracle of the oil," in which one day's supply of oil lasted for eight days is celebrated. In memory of this miracle foods are eaten that have been cooked in oil, like *latkes* (potato pancakes) and doughnuts.

Sweet foods

Another Jewish festival, Rosh Hashanah, uses food in a way similar to other religions. This is the New Year festival, and it is customary to eat honey in the hope that the new year will be sweet. Hindus also eat sweet foods at festival times. The sweet taste of the food is symbolic of the sweetness of the time that a festival, such as **Dewali**, recalls. The birthdays of many of the

Above At Rosh Hashanah Jews often dip apples in honey and say, "May it be your will, Lord our God and God of our fathers, to renew unto us a good and pleasant year."

Left The Hindu Dewali festival is celebrated at the family shrine with lighted candles and sweet foods.

gods are remembered by eating sweet things. The god Krishna liked molasses as a child, so on his birthday, many worshipers will eat molasses on pancakes made from yogurt and honey. The special *prasad* offered to the god Rama on his birthday may also be made from molasses.

People also eat sweet things during many Muslim festivals. The birthday of the prophet Muhammad is celebrated by a special gathering where Muslims eat traditional sweets. A Muslim prayer expresses thanks for good food that is eaten at Id-al-Fitr: "O Lord, send down to us food from heaven so that it becomes a day of rejoicing." Id-al-Fitr is the celebration at the end of Ramadan (the month of fasting). It lasts for three days. During Id-al-Fitr Muslims visit relatives and friends. Together they eat special foods that have been prepared.

Right A Muslim family in China celebrates the end of Ramadan by eating special biscuits.

When not to eat

Some people prepare themselves for a festival by fasting. The word "fast" means that a person is not eating. A fast may go on for any length of time or during certain parts of the day, or it may mean that just certain foods are not eaten. Some fasts are compulsory for all believers, and others are optional.

Have you ever done without something for a special reason? Maybe you have saved your pocket money to buy something for someone special. Religious people make a similar kind of **sacrifice** when they give up eating for a time. They feel that going without food at particular times can be a form of worship.

Left Samina shows her class how she will break her fast with a glass of water and a date.

A time to fast

Muslims fast during the month of Ramadan. They do not eat or drink anything during the day, from sunrise to sunset. This is a compulsory fast that everyone does if they are old enough and fit enough. Young children learn how to fast by going without sweets or snacks between meals and gradually build up to going without one meal a day. It can be very hard for Muslims living in hot countries to go without water during the day. When the fast is broken at sunset each day, most Muslims follow the example of the prophet Muhammad and eat a date with some water. This is followed by a full meal. It is also recommended that all Muslims eat a nourshing meal early in the morning before sunrise.

Right Before the *iftar* meal, which breaks the fast every evening during Ramadan, a special prayer is said: "God, I have fasted for you, and I have believed in you, and with your food I break the fast."

This fast, which is called *Sawm,* is one of the **five pillars of Islam.** Fasting helps Muslims realize their dependence on Allah, and show that they are prepared for any suffering that may follow from obeying Allah. Fasting brings the community together, since all Muslims, rich and poor, share the same experience. It also helps those who usually eat well to remember what it feels like to be hungry, so they will think to help those in need.

Yom Kippur is a required fast for Jews. It lasts for one whole day, from sunset to sunset. This is the day when Jews feel they are closest to God. They start preparing for Yom Kippur ten days earlier, at Rosh Hashanah. As the first day of the New Year, it is a good time for people to look back on the past year and think about their wrongdoing. By the time of Yom Kippur ten days later, Jews should feel that they have put right all their wrongs so they can stand close to God and confess their sins. Fasting is seen as an aid to worship because it takes away the need to spend time preparing and eating food. The day of Yom Kippur is so special that every minute should be spent in prayer.

Other religions give up certain foods for a special reason. Lent is a time when many Christians give up rich foods to remember the time when Jesus fasted in

Samina, a Muslim girl, aged nine:
"This is the party we had for Id-al-fitr. It is a big celebration at the end of Ramadan. During Ramadan we are not supposed to eat anything during the day. I had one meal a day, because I'm only nine, and my little sister ate normally, except she didn't have any cookies or candy. At the party we ate the sweets we couldn't have during Ramadan."

the wilderness. **Orthodox Christians** may give up all meat and animal products at this time. This helps them to think about the time that Jesus was tempted in the wilderness, and his sacrifice of dying for them on the cross.

Hindus can choose whether to take part in fasts. Many fast before a festival and break their fast by eating the special food that has been offered to the gods for that festival. In some cases, particular foods will be avoided, such as cereals, meat, and eggs. By giving up such ordinary foods Hindus feel they are keeping pure, and the festival foods are made special.

Below Many Buddhists carry out good deeds by offering food to the monks.

Glossary

Ancestors   People far back in a family's history.

Blessings   Special words that are said to make something holy.

Castes   Social groups into which Hindu society is divided.

Chappati   A small cake of flat bread.

Communal   Shared

Dewali   The Hindu Festival of Lights.

Eucharist   A Christian thanksgiving meal, when people remember Jesus's last supper.

Exodus   The Jew's escape from slavery in Egypt; a mass departure.

Five pillars of Islam   The five most important practices for Muslims.

Grace   Words that Christians say before a meal to thank God for the food.

Gurdwara   A Sikh temple.

Gurus   Hindu or Sikh religious teachers or leaders.

Halal   Food that is prepared according to Islamic law.

Haram   Food that is not permitted according to Islamic law.

Incense   A spice that is burned to produce a sweet smell.

Kosher   Food that is "clean" according to Jewish law.

Manger   A box from which animals feed.

Orthodox Christians Members of the Christian Church based mainly in Eastern Europe.

Orthodox Jews   Jews who strictly follow the teachings God revealed to the prophet Moses.

Prasad   Food which has been blessed for Hindus.

Purified   Made very clean.

Resurrection   The Christian belief that Jesus came back to life after his death.

Sacrifice   To give up something important, mainly for religious reasons.

Slaughter   The killing of animals, especially for food.

Symbolizes   Represents or stands for something else.

Vegetarians   People who do not eat meat.

Books to read

Barbarians, Christians, and Muslims (Minneapolis: Lerner Publications, 1975)

Buddhist Festivals (Vero Beach, Fl.: Rourke Corp., 1987)

Christian Celebrations for Autumn & Winter (Carthage, Ill.: Good Apple, 1990)

Jewish Days and Holidays (Bellmore, N.Y.: Adama Publications, 1986)

Many Children: Religions Around the World (Reston, Va.: M.A. Thomas, 1987)

Religion and Society (Milwaukee: Gareth Stevens Inc., 1991)

Sikh Festivals (Vero Beach, Fl.: Rourke Corp., 1993)

Picture acknowledgments

The publishers wish to thank the following for supplying the photographs in this book:
J. Allan Cash 7, 8; John Chorley/University of Wolverhampton 5, 13, 15 top, 17, 22, 26; Eye Ubiquitous 10 (Paul Seheult), 28 (Peter Sanders), 29 (Paul Thompson); Format Partners Photo Library 15 bottom (Maggie Murrary), 16 (Judy Harrison); Hutchison Library 12, 21 top (Liba Taylor), 24 both (top, Liba Taylor); Life File 6 (M. Maidment), 9 (Nicola Sutton); Christine Osborne Pictures 18, 19, 20, 27; The Regional R.E. Centre (Westhill College) & Stanley Thornes 23; Skjold Picutres 14; Wayland Picture Library 11 (Jimmy Holmes), 21 bottom (A. Hasson), 25 (Julia Waterlow).

Index

Numbers in **bold** indicate photographs

blessings 13
Buddhists 7, **7, 29**

Christians 8, 14, **14,** 19–20, 22,
    22, 28
Christmas 22
cows 4, 7, 9, **9**

Dewali 24

Easter 22–23

fasting 5, 26–29
food laws 6–7, 9, 12

grace 14, **14**
gurdwara 12, 14, 18, **18**
Gurus, Sikh 8, 18

halal food 4, **5,** 9, 10, **10**
haram food 9, 10
Hindus 4, 7–8, 10–11, **11,** 14,
    15, **15, 16,** 16–17, 24, **24,** 29
Holy Communion 19–20, **20**

Id-al-Fitr 25, 28 **28**

Jesus 14, 19–20, 22–23, 28–29
Jews 4, 8, 9, 10, 12, 13, 20–21,
    23–24, **24,** 28

karah parshad 18, **19**
kosher food 4, 10

Lent 28–29

Muhammad 27
Muslims 4, 8, 9, 10, 12, 15, 25,
    25, 26, 27–28, **27, 28**

Orthodox Christians 29
Orthodox Jews 13

Passover 12, 23, **23**
prasad 17, 25
prayers 9, 10, 11, 13, 14–15, 18

Ramadan 25, 27–28
Roman Catholics 4, 20
Rosh Hashanah 24, **24,** 28

St. Peter 8
Shabbat 20–21, **21**
sharing 16, 17–19
Sikhs 4, 8, 10, 11, 12, **12, 13,**
    14, 15, 17–19
sweet food 24–25

Torah 9

vegetarians **5,** 7, 17

washing 11, 13, **13,** 15

Yom Kippur 28